A JOURNEY WITHIN

HEELOLY UPASANI

"My beloved father and mother"

Contents

Foreword — *vii*

Preface — *ix*

Acknowledgements — *xi*

Prologue — *xiii*

1. Precious Gems Of Life — 1
2. Time, The Golden Chance — 2
3. The Future Is Unseen — 3
4. Fortune — 4
5. Failure — 5
6. The Sound Of Silence — 6
7. Let Me Be Me — 7
8. Crazy For My Dreams — 8
9. Attitude Has Many Ways To Be Seen — 9
10. The Power Of A Smile — 10
11. My Life Is Mine — 11
12. Why Should I Stop? — 12
13. Why I Change Myself? — 14
14. I Am Different, So I Am Unique — 16
15. My Inner Child — 17
16. Loneliness Is Not My Happiness — 18
17. My Smile Is My Expression — 19
18. My Free Moment — 21
19. Every End Sparks A Beginning — 22
20. Beyond The Dark Phase — 23

Contents

21. Life Is About Our Dreams   24

22. The Flight Of Desire   26

23. They Say And Say   27

24. What's Truly Precious To Me   28

25. Let's Be Crazy   29

26. My Brother   30

27. True Love   32

28. Life Or Friend, Who Is Friend?   33

29. Thanks To The Lord Of Lords   35

30. When My Eyes Are Closed   36

31. When I Get Hurt, I Get Success   38

32. Embrace Before Sleep   39

33. The Last Breath   40

Thank You   41

Foreword

"A Journey Within" is a poetic reflection on life's emotions, challenges, and dreams.

Through these verses, I invite you to explore the depth of human experiences—love, resilience, hope, and self-discovery.

May these words resonate with your soul and accompany you on your own journey within.

Preface

This collection was born from my thoughts, experiences, and emotions.

Each poem carries a piece of my heart, capturing the beauty of life's uncertainties, the strength in struggles, and the love that defines us.

I hope these words find a place in your heart and inspire you to embrace your journey.

Acknowledgements

I extend my heartfelt gratitude to my family, whose love and support have shaped me.

To my friends, who have encouraged me to follow my passion, and to every reader who takes the time to immerse themselves in my words—thank you.

This book is for you.

Prologue

Life is a collection of moments—some fleeting, some eternal.

Through poetry, I seek to capture the emotions that define our existence.

This book is not just about words; it is about the journey, the struggles, and the beauty we often overlook.

Let these poems be a mirror to your own soul.

1. Precious Gems of Life

Life is like a seed.
It grows and flourishes through actions.
It spreads wide, giving shade.
But there are rocks and pebbles along the way.
Some rocks can make you strong.
Others will shape you in time.
Some give a quick helping hand.
While a few lend their steady support.
Some will show real kindness.
But true friends are rare and sincere.
Hold onto them and never let go.
They are the treasures of your heart.

2. Time, the Golden Chance

It will arrive like leaves in the wind.
And leave like a storm, ferocious and swift,
But the impact it has won't ever fade away.
It's up to you to recognize the call,
Since you will have to start over from the beginning if you don't.
But if you take the chance and grab it,
Time will propel you onward in the dance of life.
Enjoy every minute and don't let it pass you by
Since time is something that can never be recovered.

3. The Future Is Unseen

Do I know what's ahead, the path I must take?
Do I know the obstacles or the opportunities I'll face?
Do I know when success will occur or
How long it will take to overcome?
Do I know the steps in my life's journey?
The turns and twists, the lessons to be learned?
The fact is, I have no certainty other than
That perseverance will lead to success.
Despite the uncertain future, I will persevere,
As each stride leads me closer to the sunrise.

4. Fortune

*Fortune is a mysterious power that no one can fully understand
or bring.
The route is unpredictable,
Yet the seeds are sowed in just one moment.
Happiness may give way to grief, and at last,
Seriousness might evolve into crazy.
At the whim of fortune, mood shifts;
It's a never-ending dance of fate.
While the idler may spot opportunities,
The dedicated person may not locate the path.
Moments in life test our mental faculties,
But a cheerful outlook aids in overcoming them.
We must remain optimistic despite our uncertainties and
anxieties
Because optimism brings us to the light of fortune.*

5. Failure

What is the definition of failure on the path to success,
Especially when starting out?
We embrace failure as the first lesson
When stones and gravel obstruct your initial step.
When ambition beckons but indolence prevents it,
The wait is entirely your fault.
Nobody else can stop you or bring you down;
If you persevere, you can overcome failure and achieve success.
Like a tiny bird that is incapable of flying,
It rises after falling and reaches for the sky.
Every setback fuels your drive and ignites your goals,
Teaching and inspiring you.
Embrace the fight and don't be afraid to fail,
Since it creates strength to overcome challenges.

6. The Sound of Silence

Sound is the single most powerful force in the world,
Disclosing truths about reality.
Harsh sounds may cause pain, make you flinch,
While the soft coil of love is deepened by sweet sound.
The bonds of friendship are reinforced by protective sound,
And others' concern is evident.
Every sound has an impact,
Whether it be one of love, pain, or ease,
But the sound of silence is the most distinctive.
Silence expresses what words cannot,
Exposing our suffering on a deeper level.
Eyes may waver, revealing our sorrow,
But stillness reveals the reality and provides solace.
The purest, most lucid representation of the heart's
Intent is the sound of quiet.
We discover the actual, the real,
And a way to fully comprehend intentions in quiet.

7. Let Me Be Me

Let the fragnance of flowers shape my mood,
Let the spectrum of rainbow define my attitude.
Let me just be myself for a second—
Wild and free, carefree and real.
Allow me to trip and fall, laugh, and accept everything.
Allow me to shine, despite my clumsiness and bubbliness.
No fights to fight, no tears to cry,
No terror of the night, and no rage of the day.
For a minute, let me be myself
Without worrying about loss or burdens.

8. Crazy for My Dreams

I'm crazy about want to be as bright as the sun at the end of the day.
I'm crazy about pursuing my goal.
To live my dreams wholeheartedly.
Regardless of what others say,
I will not let them hinder my progress.
I believe that I will become everything
That I am meant to be.
I'll keep my dreams alive inside of them
As they concentrate on their own pace.
It's only a matter of time till I reach my star,
And I know that the road I pick is mine.

9. Attitude Has Many Ways to Be Seen

Every view has something to say,
Thereby one thing can't be seen with solely one manner.
That is a virtue in our attitude.
To view events with strength instead of grief.
While one moment seems complex,
With careful thought, we can solve the next.
Keeping up with life's demands requires strong willpower.
A strong attitude leads to willpower,
Helping by drive early in difficult phases.
While some may view attitude as a defect or a root of conflict,
It's simply the key to realizing the light.
Too much attitude can make people laugh,
Let out a sneer, and make them afraid.
A calm attitude permits us to solve issues,
Overcome challenges, and seize openings.
Our attitude is key , as it defines the way we embrace life's
hardships.

10. The Power of a Smile

There's a cheery smile,
A smile that wipes tears.
There's a joyful smile,
And one of mercy, both pure and coy.
A smile of contentment is evident.
An expression of gratitude through a smile.
It's difficult to discover the genuine smile,
Though, the one that radiates calm.
It's the smile you keep even when you have nothing else.
A light of hope and a calm refrain,
Welcoming fresh opportunities to grow and gain.

11. My Life Is Mine

My life is mine to lead, and nobody has the right to choose how I
shine.
No one can modify my dreams or dictate what I should do.
My picks are my own, and I choose to live freely.
I will endeavor to achieve my goals
Without being discouraged by judgment or doubt.
The criticism and bids to hinder
My progress will prove insignificant in the long run.
They may first dispute and postpone,
But if I thrive, they will alter their minds.
Forgetting the doubts they expressed in past times,
Folks will show me support and gratitude.
If I give up on my path for others' opinions,
I will be left with no options.
I'll stay focused, steadfast, and loyal.
My goal is clear and I know what to do.
I will establish my worth and silence their claims.
My life is my own, and I won't play their games.
My life is wholly mine and cannot be judged or limited by
others.

12. Why Should I Stop?

Why should I put my life aside due to the opinions of others?
Why should I stop my dreams, my hues?
Why should I adjust my goals to fit someone else's ideal life?
Why do they have to decide for me?
Why let their opinion taint my truth?
Why should I be pushed to my limits by others' opinions?
Why should I alter my routine or style
Based on the opinions of others?
When my delight is meant to be born,
Why should I mourn for their disdain?
They say things that I don't want,
So I won't stop my goals, my fire, or my desires.
They're imperfect and lack true vision.
They should reflect before passing judgment on me.
My heart cannot be broken, my confidence destroyed,
Or me torn apart by anyone.
I'll value those who inspire and glean,
And I'll avoid those who seek to degrade.
Why shouldn't I grin if it helps me relax?
Why shouldn't I cry if it brings me relief?
I will live my life as I see fit, no matter what.
Why should I stop? For my dreams, my freedom,

And my bright light, I will stand and fight.

13. Why I Change Myself?

You might wonder why I alter myself for other people.
Is it because they want me to wear a different mask?
I'm told I'm not good enough,
Therefore I try to change to match their expectations.
My preferences and my ways alter, but why?
I begin to swing due to the opinions of others.
They dislike the way I live and the way I dress,
But I've come to realize that
Why I should give is my happiness.
Only a small number first urge me to change,
But eventually, they start to pour in.
To fit their perspective, they want me to change,
But I know deep down that's not the case.
They seek to change my behavior and core,
But I see this is not my purpose.
I would comply if their demands were helpful for me,
But I don't strive to change for other people.
I am content with myself and don't feel the need to hide.
I'll never regret my happiness,
And I won't let anyone else make me forget that.

I pledge to remain true to myself and not alter for others.

14. I Am Different, So I Am Unique

While it's true that I'm unique,
I believe that being different is what defines me.
They don't share my preferences,
So why should I try to fit in or compete with them?
What I can do, they may not achieve,
Yet they think they are perfect its hard to believe.
No one is whole, and
Perfection is a fiction that cannot be achieved.
Their pals share similar interests
And expect me to comply and obey.
The world is huge, and each individual is unique.
There is no need to criticize our nature or choices.
It's very reasonable that their perspective, mannerisms,
And style differ from mine.
Where would life be if everyone were the same?
Our individuality is shaped by our differences.
If others do not listen or see,
I will pursue my own path and be free.
For being myself is the best i can do,
I am different, and that makes me true.

15. My Inner Child

Dear heart, I would want to share with you today the sentiments
I have held onto, both genuine and old.
With a broad smile, everyone admits that the best part of life
Is experiencing the bliss of childhood.
As a child, I had no worries about the future or concerns.
Every day was a spark, a fresh delight,
And I was brimming with happiness and vitality.
I now remember those times and long for that rush
When I sat by myself, silently, and motionless.
Once the past is gone, I can't go back,
But I can shift how I think and continue.
The world felt right in those carefree days
When there was no tension
In sight and everyone was a friend.
Despite the passage of time,
The desire to reconnect with my inner child persists.
My childhood may be long gone,
But the child inside of me will always be there.
Soon, I hope, the child will get up and play,
Bringing happiness and tranquility to make every day better.

16. Loneliness is Not My Happiness

Living alone is the route I've chosen to script my luck,
Not the way I'm stuck.
Solitude offers a chance to self-discovery and personal growth.
That's where I develop my self-confidence and
Overcome my grief and its defenses.
It's how I discover ways to seek within,
Bravely face challenges, and resist giving up.
I try to pause for a moment,
Stop the tears, and smile when things are tough.
My existence is shaped by each achievement,
Turning loneliness into power to thrive.
In alone, I rise and stand strong,
Turning my story into a victory shout.

17. My Smile is My Expression

My laugh conveys genuine delight,
And my smile conveys a variety of emotions.
"Hello," it says when I smile at other people.
A greeting that warms and strengthens ties.
When I smile alone, it has two meanings: first,
It brings back memories of loved ones,
Such as family and friends, and second,
It represents the beauty of the location I've spared.
My smile represents my soul,
Bringing delight in small times and making me whole.
It reflects my happiness, brings excitement,
And brightens everything.
A smile can calm the tension on the heart,
But eyes might convey sorrow or grief.
The secret to calming the mind and uplifting
The soul is to hear someone smile.
But it's not always obvious how to smile at difficult moments;
A modest smile might not show up or a large one might not suit.
Sometimes it's difficult to make up our minds,
But in the end, we smile proudly.

The world feels lighter when we smile,
Even though it's not always easy.

18. My Free Moment

My free moments occur when there is no
Strain, pressure, or frequent mention.
My free moment is when no one is there
To judge, comment, or make noise.
My free moment is spent doing what I enjoy,
Without any time constraints or external pressure.
When there are no comparisons and I can be myself
Without anyone's approval, it is my free moment.
It's when I'm willing to smile and feel the joy of life,
When all sadness fades away and nothing is wrong.
With no anxieties or weight on my mind,
I feel free and find peace.
When I'm at peace, letting go of stress, and finding relief,
That's when I truly enjoy life.
I'll continue to live this way, regardless of what others say.
I will follow my soul and make my own decisions
Since this is my life and I am in charge.
No one can judge or tell me what's right.
In my free moment, I'll shine bright.

19. Every End Sparks a Beginning

A fresh beginning always starts with an end,
From the depths of pain, where hearts may bend.
It could be the silent sigh of the soul or the hopes that soar.
Taking the first steps towards passion on a rocky route
Might lead to beautiful ways filled with fantasies.
To accomplish, to build, to begin again,
An end opens room for the new and true.

20. Beyond the Dark Phase

After frustration, there is a positive outcome that shines brightly.
As the dark period ends, the day will be greeted with a bright
light.
A tiny hope can grow into a strong desire.
This intense drive will direct your climb to the summit
Of accomplishment at an appointed moment.
But first, bear the deep darkness, through difficult tests,
And through persistent nights.
Only through darkness can you appreciate
The glory of a transformed and dazzling face.

21. Life Is About Our Dreams

Being born, attending school, graduating, getting a good job,
Or conforming to social norms are not the only things that
constitute life.
It goes beyond only taking care of our family and ourselves.
Only the breadth of our dreams can restrict the bounds of life.
It whispers, "Do what you truly love,"
Rather than confining us to a single course.
There is no burden to follow a script or excel
At something that doesn't align with your values.
Dreams come to visit us as we sleep at night.
Occasionally, they mirror our anxieties,
Reflecting the discomfort of chores we detest.
They often inspire us to pursue our passions
And remind us that joy leads to success.
People may encourage you to follow their path,
Claiming it will improve your status or income.
However, they hardly ever suggest going after your passion.
Rather, their will respond, "You can't do that."
These words erode confidence over time.
But if you keep at it, they'll change their tune.

They will say, "I always told them to follow their dreams," once
you achieve success.
They will lie and claim credit for your bravery.
However, don't allow their skepticism divert you.
Perseverance is the key to success,
So keep practicing and improving your skills.
Follow your dreams because they are all yours,
And you will succeed if you are determined to do so.

22. The Flight of Desire

When the darkness's brilliance descends over you
And it seems like there is nothing left to do,
When hurdles arise and riddles confuse,
You'll feel the weight of what you've lost.
Tears will fall from your tired eyes
Due to the hustle and bustle and constant crying.
You will fall further from grace,
Yet your deep longing will keep you on as well.
A strong and brilliant fire can lead you through even the longest
night.
The flight of desire will lift you higher,
And the goal you seek will be within reach—
A destiny fulfilled via what you teach—
Because your soul will not tire despite the fall.

23. They Say and Say

People keep saying exactly the same thing:
They observe you daily from distance.
They simply talk, though,
While their words are loud, their deeds are feeble.
They won't step in or lend a helping hand;
Instead, they will watch you take a stance.
Their talks never stop, but stay aware this:
They aren't your true companions.
Don't let folks' remarks tie you back or hurt you.
Their remarks won't bring you joy or sorrow,
But they vary from day to day.

24. What's Truly Precious to Me

Some sense their gems to be precious and bright,
While others find joy in their outfits.
Some love their smile and face,
While others cherish their jewelry and sense of style.
Some individuals value the status
And wealth linked with the riches.
Love, rather than riches or gain,
Has the power to heal and soothe pain.
The embrace of friends and family,
A connection that no sort of treasure will ever replace.
To be free is the greatest value,
And this is the most priceless gift I have ever seen.

25. Let's Be Crazy

Let's be crazy for the joy of laughing,
For the desire for achievement that keeps us going.
Let's feel angry for defying our hearts and standing away.
Let's be crazy for living without fear
And for savoring every moment of life.
Let's be angry for paving our own path
And creating a life that is uniquely ours every day.
Let's be crazy for starting over
And realizing our ambitious goals.
Allow the chaos to generate a passion
That drives our ongoing fight.

26. My Brother

My brother, a mystery I will never fully understand,
Is both my rival and my best friend at times.
Nobody really gets his behavior;
He always gripes about me, but his love never wavers.
He tells his pals,
"My sister's so naughty, she never listens and never does what I
want, truly."
However, he becomes quite defensive and angry
If someone dares to criticize me.
"Leave me alone, you drive me insane!"
He complains when I say, "Come, brother, let's play again!"
How come you can't leave? Let me rest in peace!
In his heart, however, his love never stops.
Then, one day, frustrated,
I say, "All right, I'll stay away and not bother you."
Keep in mind that you are still a member of my family,
And I will leave you alone.
The silence deepens, but can he stand it?
Because the heart of a brother is pure and loving.
Even if they are not expressed,
He will make an effort to repair what has been damaged with
acts of love.

When the day arrives when I'm dressed as a bride, he can't help
but cry.
"Look after my sister," he begs sincerely, "she's kind and sweet;
meet her needs."
Because she is the greatest sister in the world to me,
Let her pursue her ambitions and be free.
Though brothers rarely express their true feelings,
They are distinguished by their affection for their sisters.
Though sisters express their emotions with ease,
A brother's love is like a quiet breeze- steady, unwavering,
Always there,
A bond of love beyond compare.

27. True Love

For me, a lover isn't the key to true love.
My brother is my genuine love.
He binds me to his care, loves me without conditions,
And defends me—even when he's upset.
You are the shield that keeps me safe when our parents scold me.
You bring me joy and brightness into the room
By making me laugh when I'm feeling depressed.
You stand by my side constantly and play with me.
The world's greatest is you, brother.
Although every sister adores her brother,
You are the greatest person in my view.
You are my anchor and constant;
You share your world with me and have never wounded my
feelings.
You can be a rival or a friend at different times,
But nobody knows you as well as I do.
Your love and gifts never cease to amaze me.
How could I ever tally all the ways you've expressed your concern?
Because you're constantly there, I never feel afraid or alone.
You are my constant companion in both happiness and illness.
My sibling,Never change.
You are the center of my universe and my real love.

28. Life or Friend, Who Is Friend?

It is frequently said that "life is our best friend."
However, a moment later, they leave with their companions.
How can we know who our best buddy is?
While life lays out the course we must take,
A friend grants us the flexibility to choose how to go.
A buddy is there to support us through every hardship that life throws at us,
Testing our fortitude and determination.
Life develops our aspirations and presents us with two options:
A good path and a terrible one.
Our friends are the ones who assist us in choosing virtue over vice.
Life, along with a true friend, reminds us of the path forward,
Even when we veer off course.
Life and our friends care for us without conditions,
And neither evaluates us based on our riches or beauty.
A buddy and life encourage us without ever discouraging or leaving us.
They are both irreplaceable in their own special ways.
Because a friend illuminates the path, and life shapes our path.

They complete us, so there's no need to compare them.

29. Thanks to the Lord of Lords

Thank you, Lord of Lords,
For not granting me endless accords.
For sleepless nights, unanswered prayers, darkness, and sorrow.
Thank you, Lord of Lords,
For the tears that helped strengthen my cords.
Thanks to you,
I've learnt to soar and discover contentment.
Thanks to you,
I've overcome the darkness and transformed my shadows into
light.
Every day is a brighter smile thanks to the challenges I've
overcome.
Thank you to the Lord of Lords.

30. When My Eyes Are Closed

When I close my eyes,

My mind wanders and

My imagination blossoms in the darkness.

I watch as clear, vibrant visuals appear

When my heart becomes patient and fear is banished.

Anger disappears during those times,

And a soft breeze that is as light as day touches me.

I remember things I've done and

My life's purpose while my eyes are closed.

In the quiet, the darkness seems serene,

And my heart beats rapidly as it finds its comfort.

Since no one can see,

There is no need to be afraid at night.

Even if I'm crying uncontrollably,

My smile remains alive.

I experience the grace of nature and recall the beauty

Of every moment while my eyes are closed.

The people I care about, the love I've experienced,

The accomplishments I've made, and the seeds I've planted.

As I see those moments when I've accomplished my objective,

I experience inner joy.
When my eyes are closed, I discover calm within.
A feeling of joy I can't disguise.
Because when my eyes are closed,
I feel incredibly fortunate as my heart and mind rest in the
silence.

31. When I Get Hurt, I Get Success

Every time I try anything new, it's not flawless.
I make mistakes and trip and fall.
"Next time, I'll get it right," I assure myself.
Once more, though, errors remain visible.
I dwell on my shortcomings and contrast them with others,
Feeling upset by their perfection.
In despair, I pause and let uncertainty to rule my thoughts,
But I later come to the realization that's not what I need.
I promise that rather than feeling depressed,
I should carefully examine and watch as the errors gradually decrease.
With every effort, I develop and get better.
I start moving forward little by little.
So going forward, when I try something new,
I'll consider my own opinion rather than that of others.
I'll accept my pace and avoid comparisons
Since I'll discover my grace by my blunders.
I'll accomplish my goals one day since learning,
Not a select few, is the key to success.

32. Embrace Before Sleep

Let me be embraced by death before I am wrapped up by sleep,
And let me treasure the comforting warmth of affection.
Let pending promises be fulfilled before falling asleep.
To fulfill certain dreams,
It's important to sleep with a satisfied grin
And without suffering or regret.
In the end, it's just me and my sleep.
May I stay in the hearts of my loved ones,
Forgive everyone, and be forgiven.

33. The Last Breath

When I drew my first breath,
I was filled with joy and tears.
But when I take my last breath,
I hope it fills me with happiness.
When my eyes blink, they embrace brightness.
Even after a lengthy sleep,
I hope to smile at the brightness.
Either the lovely falsehood and the painful truth are known to
me,
And I'm not trying to avoid either.
Let me live blissfully despite the painful falsehood, for when I
fall asleep,
The truth will remain true and I will be able to sleep pain-free.

Thank You

As this journey of words comes to an end, I hope these poems have touched your heart, sparked introspection, and reminded you of the strength within.

May you continue to dream, love, and embrace every moment with courage and grace.

The journey within never truly ends—it only evolves.

9 798889 744006 1